CHAKRAS FOR BEGINNERS

A Practical Guide to Radiate Energy, Heal and Balance Yourself Through the Power of Chakras

ALEXANDER YAMASHITA

CHAKRAS FOR BEGINNERS
Copyright © 2015 by Alexander Yamashita.
All rights reserved.

This document is geared towards providing exact and reliable information in regards to the topic and issue covered. The publication is sold with the idea that the publisher is not required to render accounting, officially permitted, or otherwise, qualified services. If advice is necessary, legal or professional, a practiced individual in the profession should be ordered.

From a Declaration of Principles which was accepted and approved equally by a Committee of the American Bar Association and a Committee of Publishers and Associations.

In no way is it legal to reproduce, duplicate, or transmit any part of this document in either electronic means or in printed format. Recording of this publication is strictly prohibited and any storage of this document is not allowed unless with written permission from the publisher. All rights reserved.

The information provided herein is stated to be truthful and consistent, in that any liability, in terms of inattention or otherwise, by any usage or abuse of any policies, processes, or directions contained within is the solitary and utter responsibility of the recipient reader. Under no circumstances will any legal responsibility or blame be held against the publisher for any reparation, damages, or monetary loss due to the information herein, either directly or indirectly.

Respective authors own all copyrights not held by the publisher.

The information herein is offered for informational purposes solely, and is universal as so. The presentation of the information is without contract or any type of guarantee assurance.

The trademarks that are used are without any consent, and the publication of the trademark is without permission or backing by the trademark owner. All trademarks and brands within this book are for clarifying purposes only and are the owned by the owners themselves, not affiliated with this document.

TABLE OF CONTENTS

Introduction 4
Chapter 01: *An Overview on Chakra* 5
Chapter 02: *Six Techniques to Balance your Root Chakra* 10
Chapter 03: *Six Techniques to Balance Your Sacral Chakra* .. 12
Chapter 04: *Eight Ways on Balancing your Plexus Chakra* 14
Chapter 05: *Five Techniques on Balancing Your Heart Chakra* 16
Chapter 06: *Six Ways of Balancing Your Throat Chakra* 18
Chapter 07: *Seven Techniques in Balancing Your Third Eye Chakra* 20
Chapter 08: *3 Ways to Balance your Crown Chakra* 22
Chapter 09: *Chakra Energy Centers* 24
Chapter 10: *Benefits of Balancing Your Chakras* 31
Chapter 11: *Three Influential Chakra Experts That You Should Look Up To* 34
Chapter 12: *Five Chakra Music Albums To Listen While Balancing Your Chakras* 37
Chapter 13: *Frequently Asked Questions* 40
Conclusion 43
Check Out My Other Books 44

INTRODUCTION

I want to thank you and congratulate you for downloading the book, *Chakras For Beginners: A Practical Guide To Radiate Energy, Heal And Balance Yourself Through The Power Of Chakras.*

This book contains proven steps and strategies on how to heal and balance yourself through fourteen powerful chakras recommended by experts. In the first chapter, we'll discuss an overview of what chakra is – including its seven systems that you can use in your daily life.

Other highlights of this *Chakras for Beginners* book are various techniques in balancing the said systems, an in-depth explanation on chakra energy centers and 21 proven benefits of balancing your chakras.

Thanks again for downloading this book,
I hope you enjoy it!
Alexander Yamashita

CHAPTER 01:
AN OVERVIEW ON CHAKRA

Chakras (or "Chakra") are systems of knots or energy points in the body that provide vital energy during meditation. Chakras are believed to be parts of not just the "physical body", but also its meeting points referred to as *Nadiis*. The types of chakras are presented based on scriptural teachings or texts, with the *Tantric* being the most commonly used today. Chakra was derived from the Sanskrit words "Turning" and "Wheel". In the *Yogic* context, chakra means "Whirlpool" and "Vortex".

Characteristics of Chakra
Ancient Hinduism and Buddhism teachings present a variety of chakras. According to meditation expert David White, the body's response to other physical structures is considered a form of chakra. "There is no particular standard in chakra systems. Every school or every teacher has their own system", White added.

Other characteristics of chakra are:

- They are mainly associated with a series of deities and colors like the *Mantra-Seed* syllable.
- They possess a series of "spokes" or "petals".
- Its two-sided channels often cross the chakra's "center channel" during meditation.
- They are situated at the *Shusunma* or center channel.
- They form a specific body part, along with the *Vayus* (winds), Nadiis and breath channels.

Chakra Systems in the 20th Century
White traces the history of chakra in the 20th century from Arthur Avalon's critically acclaimed book *The Serpent Power*

(in which the *Satcakranirupana* was introduced). Explained below are seven chakra systems applicable in today's generation. These systems are connected to *Vasu*, an elemental deity that symbolizes material elements.

Muladhara (Root Chakra)
The Muladhara is symbolized by the color red and lotus with four petals. Its center is situated at the spine's base visible in the coccygeal region. Muladhara is associated with survival, security and human instinct. It governs spirituality, sensuality and a sense of stability.

In this chakra system, the three basic Nadiis slowly separate to create an upward movement. It is where the *Kundalini* takes a rest by wrapping itself four times around the *Black Svayambhu*.

Swadhistana
Also referred to as *Adhishtana* or *Svadhistana*, the Swadhistana system is symbolized by a crescent moon-like lotus with orange petals. Its seed mantra is called *Vam* and the presiding deity is the *Brahma-Shakti*, which is often associated with the *Varuna* crocodile.

This chakra is situated along the sacrum hence it is associated with sexual energies. Swadhistana is considered as the person's genitourinary system playing a vital role in seeking pleasure and responding to sexually related emotions, addictions, violence and relationships. It governs spirituality, joy, creativity, enthusiasm and reproduction.

Manipura
Manipura (or *Manipuraka*) is symbolized by an upside-down, pointed triangle with ten yellow petals. Its seed syllable is called *Ram* while its presiding deity is called the *Braddha Rudra*.

This chakra relates to the digestive and metabolic systems. According to research, Manipura corresponds to the *Islets of Langerhans* that are distinct groups of adrenal glands and cells along the pancreas. These groups play a very important role in digestion. Manipura governs spirituality, expansiveness, personal power and proper digestion.

Anahata
Also known as *Padma-Sundara* and *Anahata-Puri*, the Anahata is symbolized by a circular flower with twelve green petals referred to as *Heartmind*. The flower appears to be a *Yantra* of two interconnected triangles, forming a hexagram. Its seed mantra is called *Yam* while the presiding deity is called the *Ishana Shiva Rudra*.

Anahata was derived from "Anartha" or thymus, which is located along the chest. Anartha is an element of the body's immune system; hence, it is responsible in warding off diseases caused by anxiety and stress.

This chakra governs well-being, rejection, equilibrium, unconditional love, tenderness, compassion and devotion to others.

Vishuddha
The Vishuddha (or *Vishuddhi*) is symbolized by a circle with 16 pale blue turquoise petals. Its seed mantra is called *Ham* while its presiding deity is called the *Panchavaktra Shiva*.

Vishuddha is associated with communication and growth in expressing one's self. Since the thyroid plays an important role in this chakra, it governs spirituality, independence, communication and sense of security.

Ajna
A lotus with two violet petals symbolizes Ajna. Considered as one of the most powerful chakra systems, its two-sided

Nadiis *Pingala* and *Ida* merge (or terminate) the Shusumna which marks the end of duality. Its seed syllable is called the OM while the presiding deity is called the *Ardhanarishvana*.

Ajna is known as the "Third Eye Chakra" since it involves the use of pineal glands that regulate the body's ability to envision things. The pineal ones are said to be the most sensitive glands for they produce melatonin during sleep. Ajna governs visual consciousness, intuition, inner guidance and trust.

Sahasrara

Literally defined as "1000-petalled lotus", Sahasrara is symbolized by a white lotus with a thousand petals located either above the crown or head. Its color represents inner wisdom.

Sahasrara relates to the pituitary glands that secrete hormones in the body's endocrine system. It governs emotional belongingness, unity, universal consciousness and mental action.

Chakra in Religious Traditions

Chakras play a significant role in the basic surviving branches of Tibetan Buddhism. Buddhists follow a series of "completion stage" practices to attain their "Buddhahood". Most *Vajrayana* experts claim that the *Avadhuti* (central channel) starts from the point of the Lord Shiva's third eye, then curves up to the head (or crown) and goes straight to the lower body parts. This results to "subtle drops" wherein the body follows a *Sanskrit* syllable.

When focusing on a particular chakra, the "subtle winds" enter the central channel. The chakra at which the subtle winds slowly enter is crucial in improving meditation practices. Meditating the "heart chakra" is essential in releasing "clearer lights" within the body while mediating the "throat chakra" is essential for lucid dreaming during sleep.

Western's Take on Chakra
In today's Western culture, chakra appears to be a concept associated with "Animal Magnetism" which aids certain illnesses. According to Franz Mesmer, the seven chakra systems were derived from the *Shakta* theory which is commonly used by Western meditation experts like Avalon and John Woodroffe.

CHAPTER 02:
SIX TECHNIQUES TO BALANCE YOUR ROOT CHAKRA

If you're quick to control your anger, you probably need to balance your root chakra. Meditation experts can attest to this: when a person's root chakra is well balanced, he/she has enough self-confidence and energy. Not to mention, the person feels more determined in pursuing his/her goals. In this chapter, we'll discuss five techniques on how to balance your root chakra.

1. **Get yourself a pedicure or foot spa**
   They say that you'll know when a person takes care of himself if his foot is clean. This technique may seem to be unusual for some, but the root chakra energy begins to regulate from the feet. That being said, pamper yourself by getting a foot spa or pedicure during weekends.
2. **Take a walk in the park**
   Focus on your feet leaving the ground as a way of connecting yourself to the world. To simply put, give yourself a break from all that stressful work and take a walk in the park.
3. **Take a shower**
   Several experts claim that taking a shower is one of the most effective root chakra cleansers. In addition to being individuals possessing a good character or intelligence, valuing our physical aspect is also important. Embrace your physicality by taking a shower everyday. It allows you to move mindfully (which is a form of meditation).

4. **Step into your yoga mat**

   Most yoga postures are effective in balancing root chakra. The "Tree Pose" is the commonly used posture here. How does it work? It's pretty simple! All you have to do is place both feet on the yoga mat then slowly bring your right foot up to form a tree-like position. Do this for 5 – 9 minutes.

5. **Dance**

   One of the best ways to balance your chakra is by dancing. You don't have to be a professional dancer to follow this technique. If you don't like others seeing you move your body, close the door and dance all by yourself. Don't forget to put in some feel-good music.

6. **See Anything "Red"**

   The root chakra is manifested by imagining or seeing anything that is "red" around you. Begin this not-too complicated meditation by placing a bright red material in front of you. Connect that material to relaxing your legs and feet.

CHAPTER 03:
SIX TECHNIQUES TO BALANCE YOUR SACRAL CHAKRA

Have you encountered a person who possesses warm friendliness without resulting to being too clingy? If so, that person is probably someone who has a balanced sacral chakra. People with strong sacral chakras have emotional stability, grounded intuition, compassion, zest for life and determination. Each of us has sacral chakra – it is located in our lower abdomen (three to four inches below the navel) and plays an important role in trust issues, hypersensitivity, emotional volatility, timidity and sexually related guilt. Hence, this chakra is the most sensitive "emotional center" of our body. If we don't take care of it, we'll experience sudden imbalances.

In this chapter are five techniques on how to balance your sacral chakra.

1. **Let go of the negativity**
   When we talk about letting go of the negativity, that means letting go of your unhealthy emotions and even relationships with people. As we let go of some things, we begin to create an energy or space for better opportunities in life.
2. **Balance other chakras if possible**
   A single imbalance in one chakra will likely affect other chakras. For example, your throat chakra is connected to your sacral chakra so when you do breathing exercises, you can feel a certain release within your throat area. That release is synonymous to balancing sacral chakra. You can also do "bridge

poses" that have a way to connect yourself with the other chakras necessary for meditation.
3. **Try visualizing anything that's "Orange"**
Orange is the color of sacral chakra, therefore when you see anything that's orange, you'll likely acquire tension-free sensibilities. For those who have joint or knee problems, sit down in a spacious area and place an orange-colored material in front of you. The next step is to visualize what that material can do to your spiritual aspect.
4. **Tone up your body**
Toning up your body allows you to let go of all the tensions and muscular gripping. It gives you extra reasons to keep your muscles healthy and strong. Having regular yoga sessions is important since it gives your body the capacity to regulate proper breathing levels (which essentially comes from the lower abdominals). You can tone up your body by doing "boat poses" or lower abdominal exercises.
5. **Do "hip-opening" yoga positions**
If you've taken regular yoga classes, you probably heard your teacher say this: "We tend to store physical and emotional tension straight from our hips, thus we do hip-opening yoga positions". If you have a doubt on the legitimacy of this technique, better try to observe where you clench or grip your muscles when caught in a stressful situation. When doing this position, keep in mind that your hips will slowly move in various directions.

CHAPTER 04:
EIGHT WAYS ON BALANCING YOUR PLEXUS CHAKRA

Do you lack self-confidence? Are you experiencing problems in your digestion? Are you having difficulty in speaking in front of people? If you say yes to these questions, you need to balance your Plexus Chakra. The latter helps the person develop a sense of self-worth. When you have a proper, well-balanced plexus chakra, you'll be able to stand up for yourself, be more determined in reaching your goals and grow as a leader (or follower).

Below are eight ways in balancing your plexus chakra:

1. Decorate your room with shades of yellow. Based from the rule of effective plexus chakra balancing, yellow is described as "energizing" and "pleasing".
2. Use lavender or rosemary scents. Both are said to grow easily in various climates; hence, this is an amazing way to apply them in your life. If you don't have these scents, you can use any essential oil.
3. Make sure your voice is clearly heard (or understood) and your necessities are taken into proper consideration. If this trick seems to be difficult for you, start with the basics.
4. Set a particular goal. Break this goal down into dissimilar yet attainable steps. Create a timeline for breaking each step. Be consistent in using your timeline as basis in setting your goal slowly but surely.
5. Make an effort to groom and dress yourself well. Hold your head high, but keep your feet on the ground. In

other words, don't be overconfident in carrying yourself.
6. Clean your messy closet (or room). If you don't have time to do this, consider other tasks that can set up your mood for relaxation.
7. Participate in any sport or physical activity.
8. Spend time relaxing under the sunlight. Go to the beach, lie down on the sands and feel the heat.

CHAPTER 05:
FIVE TECHNIQUES ON BALANCING YOUR HEART CHAKRA

Having a balanced heart chakra is one of the most beautiful feelings in the world. However, some of us (if not, most of the time) can't avoid encountering blockages at certain point of our lives. Circumstances can trigger problems within the heart – from low self-esteem to peer issues to break-ups.

A detrimental heart chakra shows a number of signs and symptoms. If not treated immediately, you'll become more defensive, suspicious, critical and afraid to let go of all things – no matter how risky they are. Get rid of this situation by following the five techniques explained below.

1. **Forgive**
   Many blockages in the heart chakra are manifested by not letting go of regret, anger, insecurity, past heartbreaks etc. In addition, the healing process will be more challenging if we seek counseling under a professional. Forgive the people who hurt you and start all over again. Focus on taking care of yourself and being more understanding towards the feelings of other people.
2. **Do yoga practice**
   A blocked heart chakra is synonymous to a blocked throat chakra, and we don't want that to happen right? Try doing the camel pose in this technique. Concentrate on elongating your body's lower back part while keeping your stretches simple by opening your upper back part.

3. **Share the love**
   One of the easiest (and best) ways to balance the heart chakra is by loving others unselfishly and unconditionally.
4. **Appreciate the people who loves you**
   Being a martyr in love is a sign of having an imbalanced heart chakra. Don't let this happen to you by allowing yourself to be loved by others. Loving yourself doesn't hurt, either!
5. **Go "Green"**
   This means that you should go outside and feel the warmth of Mother Nature. Allow the various "greens" to heal your soul.

CHAPTER 06:
SIX WAYS OF BALANCING YOUR THROAT CHAKRA

Contentment in work and artistic freedom are just some of the many factors associated with experiencing throat chakra. The latter is one of the most important "emotional centers" we need to always take care of. Keep in mind that your shoulders and ears are also associated with experiencing this chakra.

While mental and emotional issues can likely present physical signs of illnesses, being physically sick affects your chakra system. In order to get rid of this, here are six techniques you need to follow:

1. **Speak up the truth**
   Don't be afraid to tell the truth to a relative or friend. Remember this famous quote: "The truth will set you free".
2. **Pamper yourself with a massage**
   To feel better about yourself, go to a spa and spend an hour (or even more) getting a massage.
3. **Wear any jewelry you have**
   The "blue gems" found in many jewelry items are said to be associated with the throat chakra. Wear a gorgeous pair of blue necklace or earrings and carry them well.
4. **Remember, your hips don't lie**
   A damaging throat chakra affects the increase of *Kundalini*. Furthermore, the movement of our hips triggers our emotional baggage. When you'll work on those hips, make sure you have a yoga mat. Feel the

gradual release in your throat when doing "hip-friendly" poses.
5. **Drink lots of water**
Make sure that you have easy and enough access to healthy water. Drink 8 – 12 glasses everyday. Because water cleanses all the toxins triggered during digestion, drink a glass in between meals.
6. **Sing your heart out**
This amazing throat chakra cleanser doesn't need further explanations anymore. Put in some music in your player, and sing.

CHAPTER 07:
SEVEN TECHNIQUES IN BALANCING YOUR THIRD EYE CHAKRA

If your intuition is blocked due to supernatural experiences in your past (or even present), here are seven techniques on how to balance your third eye chakra.

1. **Take care of your brain health**
   The "third eye" is situated between your eyebrows or in the middle of your forehead. This is exactly where the pineal glands and brain sit. Maintain a proper brain health by eating foods rich in vitamin D. Exposure to sunlight and undergoing "fish oil diet" is also necessary.
2. **Read lots of books**
   Many believe that books are among the ultimate stress-relievers. Even in balancing your third eye chakra, gobbling on a good read lessens your worries. Do it inside your room or any place where there are no distractions.
3. **Write down your urges, dreams, hunches, feelings, smells, sensations etc.**
   You can do this in your journal or blog. If possible, share what you feel to others without looking silly.
4. **Find your own sense of wisdom**
   Take some time to sit down in a corner and find your wisdom. Seeking help (or support) from others is a great help, too! You need to connect more with your "inner knowledge" in order to be open and understanding of your own wisdom.
5. **Don't think about competition**
   Always remember this: our intuitive mind is deemed non-competitive. To simply put, people with strong

intuitive nature don't get easily swayed by competition. Let go of any "competitive energy" you're probably thinking and be happy with others' achievements.

6. **Breathe**

    Do away with over thinking and stay in a more open, neutral state. In other words, breathe. Divert yourself from the hustle and bustle of city life and relax under the warm weather coming from the outdoors.

7. **Learn from your pain and loss**

    Let go of the things that made you less of a person. Take these things as a part of your learning experience you can share with others.

CHAPTER 08:
3 WAYS TO BALANCE YOUR CROWN CHAKRA

The Crown Chakra serves as the center of positivity, happiness, inspiration, trust and devotion. It is also the center of deeper connection within others and us as well. That being said, this is one of the most important chakras we should balance everyday – and here are three ways how:

1. **Visualize**
   Visualization is one of the most effective tricks of balancing crown chakra. Take a few minutes of your own time from work and picture a yellowish orb of light placed on top of your head. Visualize that orb as something which expands or grows. Imagine that it has a way to elevate your thoughts and give you a positive feeling that you can accomplish things in your daily life.
2. **Practice your affirmations everyday**
   The practice or use of stirring affirmations gives you a well-balanced crown chakra that you truly deserve. Here's an example of an affirmation you can practice:
   I am open and innovative of my ideas.
   I believe in what is possible.
   I won't regret something I did.
   Because I know this something will make me a better person.
3. **Be inspired**
   Inspiration is something we need to become more goal-oriented. For example, think of a book you've read or concert you've been to. Keep in mind how these things made you feel as an individual. If you enjoyed that book or concert, you'll likely become

more positive, open, uplifted and inspired. Balancing your crown chakra is impossible without having a dose of inspiration.

CHAPTER 09:
CHAKRA ENERGY CENTERS

All human beings (and even animals) have a set of chakra energetic centers that are situated at the body's midline parts. These energetic centers may be well recognized in other cultures, but science and medicine have a different take on it. According to several Western studies on meditation, chakra is defined as "spinning vortices of energy in the body" which Hindu studies can attest.

Factors to Consider
A number of methods were used to help people open themselves to the idea of chakras. These methods include chanting, special diets, living in monasteries, fasting and praying. All religions often discuss the said methods, though some rarely mention the chakra energy centers because of these factors:

1. It is now very easy to open one's self to the chakras by taking nutritional supplements and eating the right amount of food. The fact about chakra as something related to the Earth's position and certain mid-points people experiences is no longer valid in the 20th century.
2. The basic obstruction in opening the chakra energetic centers is oftentimes a toxic, washed-out or sick body. Therefore, a certain level of physical and psychological health is necessary in opening the centers.
3. Some old chakra methods are no longer applicable (and recommended) in today's culture.
4. Many religious leaders don't clearly understand the significance of chakra energy centers (or even

chakras) because of their devotion to conformist views.

Chakra Energy Centers
The seven chakra energy centers are popularly known as *Lower Energy Centers* and are very concerned with the emotional and physical survival of the body. These centers are vital to the reproduction and growth of a person's "ego-self".

The First Chakra Energy Center (Root Center)
The root center is often associated with grounding and survival. Here, the person's physical structure or base is involved. Reproduction, healthy eating habits and staying intact with the environment are among the few things that relate to the root center.

How to Follow the Root Center
Color: Magenta or Red
Size: When closed, it's about 2 inches long and around 3 inches along the widest part (located below the body's anal opening). In developed or well-grounded persons, the size should grow to at least 2 feet long.
Shape: It is shaped like a funnel pointer (or less downward for beginners).
Origin: Its origin is exactly 1 ½ inches above the anal opening (which is important when standing).
Spin: Among men, the body should spin outwards then downward (counterclockwise). Among women, the body should spin inward then upward (clockwise).
Sound: AH (derived from the word *Torah*).

The root center requires a lot of work to prevent exposure to stressful lifestyles, unhealthy eating habits and toxic materials. When it's not developed, the person becomes ungrounded. Worse, his/her survival instincts will be at risk. Indeed, this chakra energy center plays a crucial role in connecting our physical aspect with the Earth by taking care of ourselves.

The Second Chakra Energy Center (Sexual Center)
The second chakra energy center has something to do with relationships, sexual relationships and gender identity.

How to Follow the Sexual Center
Color: Light or dark orange
Size: In many adults, it is around 3 inches long from the open end to the narrow end. As an individual develops, his/her sexual instincts also develop. Hence, the size can grow to 5 – 7 inches wide.
Shape: Its shape looks like two opposite narrow funnels - one opened backwards while the other is joined at the spinal cord's narrow end.
Origin: The center should start from the navel up to the spinal cord.
Spin: For men, start spinning in clockwise position. For women, do the opposite.
Sound: EE (pronounced as *eel*)

The sexual center is more beneficial among women since they have a better chakra energy center among men. In some cases, women are less confused about sex, but they give more importance to cleanliness.

The Third Chakra Energy Center (Solar Plexus)
The third chakra energy center is associated with manipulation, judgments, beliefs, and power to control one's self (or others).

How to Follow the Solar Plexus
Color: Dark or light yellow
Size: For undeveloped individuals, the size should be exactly 2 inches long from the wide end up to the narrow end. When

an individual develops in solar plexus, the size can grow to at least 4 inches.
Shape: Just like the second chakra energy, the size looks like two opposing narrow funnels – except that it has 45 to 50-degree angles.
Origin: Solar plexus' origin is around four horizontal fingers (or 2 ½ inches from the bottom of the breastbone or sternum).
Spin: For men, begin spinning counterclockwise. For women, do the opposite.
Sound: O (or something that sounds like *alone*)

Some people don't understand the importance of sharing space with others. Because of this, they likely end up in arguments or conflict with them. The golden rule of solar plexus says that we need to find our inner peace and connect ourselves with other people in a positive way.

The Fourth Chakra Energy Center (Heart Center)
The heart center involves giving importance to companionship, love and true friendship.

How to Follow the Heart Center
Color: Emerald green and dark grey
Size: When undeveloped, the size should be around 3 inches long and 3 inches wide. When a person develops, it will likely grow to a bigger size (over 7 feet wide and 10 feet long).
Shape: It looks like two opposite, funnel-shaped cones, one facing backwards and the other facing forward (think of a lotus flower with petals extended outwards from the back).
Origin: The origin is situated at the body's spinal column, above the level of the breastbone and nipples.
Spin: For men, begin spinning in clockwise position. For women, do the opposite.
Sound: OM (pronounced as *home*)

The heart center should be the easiest to balance, most especially among women. In a recent study, women have more difficulty in handling their heart chakra center due to fears of sexual manipulation by others. When the heart chakra isn't functioning properly, a person can possibly experience isolation (or being unloved) from others.

The Fifth Chakra Energy Center (Throat Center)
The throat center is connected with one's ability to show his/her talent and creativity.

How to Follow the Throat Center
Color: Dark blue
Size: For undeveloped people, the size is 1 ½ inches from the open end to the narrow end. When the person develops, the size will grow into 2 inches wide.
Shape: It looks like two opposite, medium-width funnels, each joined at its narrow ends.
Origin: It is situated at the bottom level of Adam's apple (among men) and ¾ inches away from the spinal column (among women).
Spin: For men, begin spinning counterclockwise. For women, do the opposite.
Sound: OO (or something that sounds like *hoot* or *root*)
For many people (especially women), the throat center is the only chakra energy center that isn't developing well due to thyroid-related illnesses and incapacity to share talents. When tensions occur in the neck due to falls or accidents, our throat chakra energy is affected.

The Sixth Chakra Energy Center (Third Eye Center)
Also referred to as the *Knowledge Center* or *Wisdom Center*, the third eye center mainly concerns our brain development

How to Follow the Third Eye Center
Color: Dark indigo and light purple
Size: The size varies in the third eye center. For undeveloped

people, it is around 3 – 4 inches long from wide to narrow parts. As a person develops knowledge or wisdom, the size becomes extremely long and wide.
Shape: It looks like two wide funnels – one is joined at the narrow ends while the other is extended backwards.
Origin: The third eye center begins at the pituitary glands, which is approximately located at the bottom level of the eyebrows.
Sound: I (pronounced as *eye*)
Problems concerning this chakra energy center are common in modern-day culture and progressive societies. When the third eye chakra is unbalanced, secret agendas, deceits, lies and confusion between groups of people may occur.

The Seventh Chakra Energy Center (God Center)
Also known as the *Crown Center*, the God center is connected with the person's strong connection with the divine person.

How to Follow the God Center
Color: Light violet
Size: For children, the size is usually small (not more than 3 inches long). Nonetheless, more and more babies born with God center are growing wide open. By the time they reach 30, their height and weight will change.
Shape: It looks like a narrow funnel opening from the crown up to the middle of the head.
Origin: The God center begins from the pineal gland that can be found at the middle part of the skull.
Sound: A (pronounced as *hay*)
Disturbances in God center are very common in society today, with secular thinking being the most common one. Secular thinkers don't believe in the existence of God, afterlife and cleansing of the soul. That being said, they often criticize this chakra energy center.

Impact in Relationships
In Chakra, relationships can either be used in balancing or

using energy systems frequently. Depending on how people deal with their relationship with others, the systems can either cause confusion or will make them feel better about themselves.

Aura Concept in Chakra

The aura concept is related to the seven chakra energy systems (discussed in this chapter). From the word "Aura" itself, the concept refers to the glow of human beings, animals and non-living things. The aura concept in chakra can be photographed (or measured) using *Kirlian* style and it is made up of glows from the energy fields called *subtle bodies* that help develop the person's chakra.

CHAPTER 10:
BENEFITS OF BALANCING YOUR CHAKRAS

Do you pay a lot of attention to your chakras? If your answer is yes, then that's good news! Otherwise, you need to take note of the chakra imbalances listed below. *(Tip: if you're experiencing any of these imbalances, seek help from a professional)*

Mental Imbalances
- Fear of luck
- Insecure
- Unstable
- Scattered
- Exclusion
- Disconnection from life's reality
- Lack of motivation
- Ego-centered
- Materialistic
- Dogmatic
- Overly analytical (or analyzing too much)
- Criticism
- Prejudice
- Apathy and boredom
- Unclear communication
- Indecision
- Resentment
- Jealousy

Emotional Imbalances
- Depression
- Addiction

- Moodiness
- Close hearted
- Deep sadness
- Anger
- Abusiveness towards others (and self)
- Lack of willpower
- The lack of ability to express
- Eating disorders
- The need for approval (or seeking attention)
- Low self-esteem

Physical Imbalances
- Nervous disorders
- Headaches
- Difficulty in breathing
- Eye strain
- Dental problems
- TMJ
- Heart disorders
- Thyroid problems
- Digestive problems
- Low libido levels
- Reproductive problems
- Circulatory problems
- Immune disorders
- Skin disorders
- Bowel movement or bladder issues
- Injuries caused by accidents or negligence in taking care of the body
- Back pains

Benefits of Balancing Chakras
When you balance your chakras everyday, you'll get a lot of benefits listed below:

1. Experience the power of being "fully grounded" in your spiritual, physical and psychological being.
2. Clear communication of the mind and heart.
3. Lets you tap into your willpower.
4. Live up to your "highest path" in your career.
5. Abundance from distractions affecting "inner guidance" (which is important in maintaining a strong connection with self and others).
6. Clarity in analyzing things and a focused mindset.
7. Access to your "inner wisdom".
8. Attain the art of "self-mastery" in personal and professional life.
9. Increase in personal integrity.
10. A healthier release of emotions.
11. Increase and recognize intuition.
12. Increase of strength and health in the immune system.
13. Dedication (or awareness) to your life's "highest path".
14. The ability to turn dreams into reality.
15. Ease in experiencing forgiveness and love for others and self.
16. Self-confidence in expressing and accepting yourself.
17. Access to "financial wisdom".
18. Increased determination in life.
19. Release of patterns that are deemed "non-supportive" in chakras.
20. The ability to turn weaknesses into strengths.
21. Increased openness (or awareness) to spiritual and psychic information.

CHAPTER 11:
THREE INFLUENTIAL CHAKRA EXPERTS THAT YOU SHOULD LOOK UP TO

In this chapter, we'll get to know three of the most influential chakra experts today. One is a bestselling author of over 30 books on chakra. The other one keeps herself busy talking in front of thousands and the last is an in-demand yoga instructor.

Anodea Judith
Anodea Judith is one of the world's foremost experts on chakras – from the systems to therapeutic use to interpretation in the Western culture. A founding director of *Sacred Centers*, Anodea is also a spiritual teacher and writer. Her passion for upholding the human spirit is clearly seen in her books and teachings.

Anodea is currently finishing her MA Studies in Clinical Psychology and Doctorate Studies in Health & Human Services (specializing in body/mind healing) at the University of California Los Angeles. For two decades, Anodea has been conducting a series of private healing practices all over the US.

Anodea is recognized by many for *Wheels of Life: A User's Guide To The Chakra System,* a 440-page manual she personally wrote for people who want to bring out the best in them through chakras. The first edition was released in 1987, but due to several inconsistencies found, Anodea revised the book and reissued what is known today as *Wheels of Life: Second Edition* in 1995. The book sold 300,000 copies and was translated into 15 languages.

The Chakra System
In March 2000, Anodea created a six-tape audio course entitled *The Chakra System: A Complete Course in Healing & Self-Diagnosis Through Sounds Etc*. This was later followed by *The Illuminated Chakras* (in which Anodea co-worked with her son, critically acclaimed animator Alex Wayne) and *Chakra Balancing*.

Personal Views
Unknown to many, Anodea is also a musician and has deep understanding in religion, politics, ethics and ecology. She strongly believes that there is an inherent connection between cultural and individual transformation. Anodea often emphasizes in her teachings and writings that well-balanced Chakras can be achieved by connecting ourselves with not just the heavens, but the earth as well.

Cyndi Dale
Cyndi is one of the most in-demand chakra speakers, intuitive consultants and authors today. Not everyone knows that she has a naturally intuitive personality. Hence, most of Cyndi's speeches, teachings and writings are based from her personal experiences. Aside from the aforementioned careers, she also serves as consultant for individuals and groups seeking for positive changes in their lives. Her life revolves around people who desire to motivate themselves for the better.

Books
Cyndi is the woman behind the best-selling Chakra books *Illuminating The Afterlife*, *The Littlest Christmas Star*, *Advanced Chakra Healing for Cancer Patients*, *Advanced Chakra Healing For Persons With Heart Disease*, *Attracting Your Perfect Body Through The Chakras*, *Attracting Prosperity Through The Chakras*, *Kundalini: Divine Energy, Divine Life*, *Advanced Chakra Healing: Everyday Clairvoyant* and *Advanced Chakra Healing: The 4-Pathway Approach*.

Other books Cyndi wrote are *The Subtle Body* (which gained recognition from the Publisher's Awards). The success of her Amazon recommended book was followed by *The Subtle Body: The Encyclopedia of Energetic Anatomy* and an instructional DVD entitled *The Songbird Series*.

Workshops and Seminars

For the last two decades, Cyndi has conducted workshops and seminars in over 30 countries including Scotland, Iceland, Amsterdam, UK, Argentina, Brazil, Nigeria and South Africa. Her formal training has encompassed in-depth studies in Chakra as well as Shamanism and other traditional Aztec healings. This training however, took Cyndi to the remote areas of South America. It is clearly her job to encourage people from different cultures to understand their "inner selves" through chakras.

At present, Cyndi is offering classes, trainings and apprenticeship programs at the Normandale College in Minneapolis. She's also offering *Energy Works: The Subtle Body Certificate*, a seven-class program aimed for people who want to connect themselves with healing and clairvoyance.

Valerie D'Ambrosio

Valerie is the co-founder of *Hanuman Festival*, an annual event that aims to promote the importance of Yoga and other forms of meditation among young people. Her passion lies in helping people connect themselves with their spiritual, physical and emotional being. Valerie is known for using special chakra movements such as chanting and deep breaths. As someone who gives so much value to her inner being, Valerie's ultimate wish is that "someday more people will find their inner truth by connecting wisdom to their bodies instead of torturing them."

CHAPTER 12:
FIVE CHAKRA MUSIC ALBUMS TO LISTEN WHILE BALANCING YOUR CHAKRAS

Balancing your chakras won't be a "very tranquil" experience without the accompaniment of music. Just like other meditation tricks, music plays a vital role in chakras. When you enroll in regular chakra sessions, you get to hear instrumentals with Asian-inspired elements. In line with this, you probably heard the following albums below:

Freaky Chakra vs. Single Cell Orchestra
Artist: Freaky Chakra

Freaky Chakra is a musical duo comprising of Miguel Angelo Fierro and Daum Bently. For almost ten years, the duo has become one of Chakra music's staples – never failing to jump from one genre to another. Their music is described as "Funky yet relaxing" – somewhat reminiscent of Earth Wind & Fire collaborating with Kruder & Dorfmeister. In their critically-acclaimed album *Freaky Chakra vs. Single Cell Orchestra*, the duo takes Chakra music to a "more dynamic" level with collaborations from other Chakra music artists like Jon Drukman and Eefje Kan (which are notable for their African dance beats).

Low Down Motivator
Artist: Freaky Chakra

For Trance music lovers, this album is one for the books. Also from Freaky Chakra, *Low Down Motivator* is best listened to when balancing your root chakra. Dance is one of the most powerful methods in maintaining a well-balanced chakra – and this album will tell you why. Expect 50 minutes of

Trance, Electronica and a touch of Downtempo on the latter part.

Blacklight Fantasy
Artist: Freaky Chakra

This album was released at the time Fierro took a hiatus. Because of this, loyal chakra music fans thought it's over for Freaky Chakra, but Bently took the reins of producing this album on his own and the rest, as they say, is history. *Option* magazine praised *Blacklight Fantasy* for its "monotonous yet simple time signatures that don't compromise the human senses".

Chords Of The Cosmos: Harmonies Of The Zodiac With Crystal Bowls for Chakra Healing, Meditation & Balancing
Artist: Gert Wilden, Deborah Van Dike and Crystal Voices

"The Sounds of The Stars" best describes this Chakra CD. Forget about the lengthy title since it is more than just that. The album, which recently got 4 out of 5 stars from Amazon is a testament to what a legit Chakra music is. It is a comprehensive spectrum of Chakra healing, meditation and balancing sounds that employs 12-note full scales of "crystal bowls". The latter plays a significant role in producing harmonic keys for retuning.

Tibetan Chakra Meditations
Artist: Ben Scott

Considered as one of the bestselling Chakra music albums of all time, *Tibetan Chakra Meditations* is Scott's "baptism of fire" in the genre. The album is notable for its flutes and "singing bowls" that fit well with the seven chakras and its energy centers. The first half of *Tibetan Chakra Meditations* is all about harmonics, percussions and flutes while the last part focuses on just singing bowls. This album is a perfect gift for Chakra beginners and enthusiasts. You can play it anywhere – either at home or in the office (where stress and distractions are not a rarity).

CHAPTER 13:
FREQUENTLY ASKED QUESTIONS

Q: What is the best way to balance, heal and open my chakras?
A: Meditation. Throughout centuries, meditation has always been the best way of balancing, healing and opening chakras. It has a range of benefits in so many levels. In fact, meditation is the ultimate key in chakra healing as it lets a person maximize his/her potential.

Q: What if my chakras are "out of tune", unbalanced or blocked? What Should I do?
A: Having "out of tune", unbalanced or blocked chakras can likely limit your ability to improve your emotional, spiritual, mental and physical health. To get rid of this, experts suggest that you should do chakra balancing everyday.

Q: Does modern science recognize the chakra centers?
A: Yes. Chakras are more than just metaphysical systems of meditation. In a recent study by the University of Liverpool, the chakra centers are scientifically interpreted as "frontliners" for improving human visualization.

Q: What does the cross symbol in the solar plexus chakra symbolize?
A: The cross symbol in the solar plexus chakra symbolizes your body's "center of power". The message of this symbol tells us that you have the power to choose what is better for you or others.

Q: Do animals and non-living things have chakras?
A: Yes. Animals and non-living things have a subtle body (or energy field) which is important in balancing your chakras. Some experts claim that animals have three chakra systems,

but their locations, sizes, color, shapes and origins vary regardless of their growth.

Q: Who are the creators of Chakra?
A: *Caryagiti* and *Hevajra Tantra*.

Q: Is Chakra considered a "New Age" act?
A: Yes. According to Carolyn Myss, author of the book *Anatomy Of The Spirit* (released in 1996, chakras are described as classical elements applicable to the New Age. "Every experience a person had in his life gets filtered through chakra databases that are introduced by New Age experts", Myss added.

Q: Where can I buy old chakra books?
A: You'll find hundreds of them online. If you want a hard copy, check out Amazon and eBay's selection of chakra books that are made to order via shipping.

Q: What Are "Subpersonal Chakras"?
A: Subpersonal chakras are five distinct chakra systems that involve the use of arms and feet. The five systems are: *Incarnation Point Chakra, Incarnator Chakra, Subpersonal Leadership Chakra, Earth-Centering Chakra* and *Earth Star Chakra*.

Q: Aside from traditional chakra music, what are other genres we can play when balancing our chakras?
A: You can play downtempo or deep house music when balancing your chakras. As a matter of fact, any musical genre can be applied in balancing chakras. That will depend on your mood.

Q: Is being Buddhist a requirement in enrolling at chakra schools?
A: No. Anyone, regardless of gender, race, culture or religion, can enroll at chakra schools. However, you don't necessarily

have to spend bucks for 10 or 12 formal sessions. You can balance your chakras at home or even during work breaks.

CONCLUSION

Thank you again for downloading this book!
I hope this book was able to help you to follow each technique provided. Don't forget that in chakra meditation, healing and balancing, **consistency is the key** so do it everyday.

The next step is to use these chakra systems and energy centers as motivation to love others and yourself. Keep in mind that these systems and energy centers are more than just forms of balancing; they are powerful keys to keep you sane and inspired.

Finally, if you enjoyed this book, then I'd like to ask you for a favor, would you be kind enough to leave a review for this book on Amazon? It'd be greatly appreciated!

Please leave a review for this book on Amazon!
http://www.amazon.com/dp/B00QP7SUEK

Thank you and good luck!
Alexander Yamashita

CHECK OUT MY OTHER BOOKS

Below you'll find some of my other popular books that are popular on Amazon and Kindle as well. Simply click on the links below to check them out. Alternatively, you can visit my author page on Amazon to see other work done by me.

1. *Buddhism for Beginners: A Practical Guide to Embrace Buddhism Into Your Life*
   http://www.amazon.com/dp/B00P2S5NYI
2. *Zen For Beginners: Achieve Today Your Happiness and Inner Peace with Zen Buddhism*
   http://www.amazon.com/dp/B00MBFE3IC
3. *Kundalini for Beginners: Awaken Your Kundalini Within To Heal Your Body Naturally*
   http://www.amazon.com/dp/B00PLMT0H6
4. *Reiki for Beginners: Master the Ancient Art of Reiki to Heal Yourself and Increase Your Energy*
   http://www.amazon.com/dp/B00QPDKB0K
5. *Chakras for Beginners: A Practical Guide To Radiate Energy, To Heal and Balance Yourself Through the Power of Chakras*
   http://www.amazon.com/dp/B00QP7SUEK
6. *Mindfulness For Beginners: A Practical Guide To Awakening and Finding Peace In Your Life*
   http://www.amazon.com/dp/B00RH36DIG
7. *Feng Shui For Beginners: Master The Art of Feng Shui To Bring More Balance, Harmony and Energy Flow*
   http://www.amazon.com/dp/B00RQPFGQU

CPSIA information can be obtained
at www.ICGtesting.com
Printed in the USA
LVOW04s1454100316
478621LV00042B/920/P